Suzuki

Recorder School
Volume 2
Alto Recorder Part

© 1998 Dr. Shinichi Suzuki
Sole publisher for the entire world except Japan:
Summy-Birchard Inc.
exclusively distributed by
Warner Bros. Publications
15800 N.W. 48th Avenue, Miami, Florida 33014
All rights reserved   Printed in U.S.A.

ISBN 0-87487-558-7

The Suzuki name, logo and wheel device
are trademarks of Dr. Shinichi Suzuki used
under exclusive license by Summy-Birchard, Inc.

CONTENTS

Suzuki Method
New and Effective Education in Music

Through the experience I have gained by conducting experiments in teaching young children for over fifty years, I have come to the definite conclusion that musical ability is not an inborn talent but an *ability* which can be developed. Any child, properly trained, can develop musical ability just as all children in the world have developed their ability to speak their mother tongue. Children learn the nuances of their mother tongue through repeated listening, and the same process is followed in the development of an ear for music. Every day children listen to the recordings of the music which they are studying or about to study. This listening helps them to make rapid progress. The children will begin to try their best to play as well as the performer on the recording. By this method the child will grow into an adult with fine musical sense. It is the most important training of musical ability.

Tonalization

The word "tonalization" is a new word coined to apply to instrumental training as an equivalent to vocalization in vocal training. Tonalization has produced wonderful results in instrumental education. Tonalization is the instruction given to the pupil, as she learns each new piece of music, to help her produce a beautiful tone and to use meaningful musical expression. *We must train the pupil* to develop a musical ear that permits her not only to recognize a beautiful tone, but to reproduce tone in a beautiful way, like the great artists of the past and present.

Important Points in Teaching

I. "What is the best way to help a pupil enjoy learning and practicing?" This is the principal challenge for the teacher and parents, that of motivating the child properly so that she will enjoy practicing correctly at home. They should discuss this matter together, considering and examining each case in order to help the child enjoy the lessons and practice. They should be sensitive to the state of mind of the child.

II. In addition to daily practice at home, the pupil listens to the recording of the piece she is learning, every day and as often as possible. This becomes habitual. Progress will be very rapid. Six days a week of correct practice and listening at home will be more decisive in determining the child's rate of advancement than one or two lessons a week.

III. The beginning pupil should always play without musical notation at the lessons. This is the most important factor in improving the pupil's memory. It also speeds up the pupil's progress.

Instruction in music reading should be given according to the pupil's age and capability. It is very important for the pupil to learn to read notation well, but if the child is forced to simultaneously read and play music notation at the very outset of her study, and always practices with music notation, she will, in performance feel quite uneasy playing from memory and therefore will not be able to show her full ability.

In acquiring a skill, ability grows through daily habit. In learning her mother tongue, the child begins to read only after she is able to speak. The same approach should be followed in music. Simultaneous playing, while reading music notation is taught only after the child's musical sensitivity, playing skill, and memory have been sufficiently trained. In the beginning, music note reading is learned *separately* from tone production and technique.

IV. When a pupil gets to the stage where she can play a piece without a mistake in notes or fingering, the time is ripe for cultivating her musicianship. I would say to the child, "Now you are ready. We can start very important work to develop your ability," and then I would proceed to teach beautiful tone, fine phrasing, and musical sensitivity. The quality of the pupil's performance depends greatly on the teacher's constant attention to these important musical points.

The following point is very important. When the child can perform piece A satisfactorily and is given a new piece, B, she should not drop A but practice both A and B. This procedure should continue as new pieces are added. She should always be reviewing pieces that she knows well in order to develop her ability to a higher degree.

V. Parents and children always watch individual lessons of other children. This is an added motivation. When the child hears music played well by other children, she will want to be able to play as well, and so her desire to practice will increase.

Lessons should vary in length according to the need of the child. The attention span of the child should be taken into account. If the small child is able to concentrate only for a short time, it is better to shorten the lesson time until she is more adaptable. At one time the lesson may be only five minutes, at another, thirty minutes. Teachers work with the parents and the children.

Shinichi Suzuki

EL MÈTODO SUZUKI DE FLAUTA DULCE
MÈtodo Nuevo, Educativo y Eficaz

A través de la experiencia que he acumulado trabajando en la enseñanza de los niños pequeños por mas de 50 años, he llegado a la conclusión que la habilidad musical no es un talento innato, sino que puede ser desarrollada. Cualquier niño con el entrenamiento adecuado puede lograrlo, de la misma forma en que todos los niños del mundo han desarrollado la habilidad de hablar su lengua materna. Ellos aprenden los diferentes matices de su idioma por la constante repetición, proceso similar que se sigue para el entrenamiento de su oído musical. Diariamente deben escuchar las grabaciones de la música que están estudiando o van a estudiar. Esto les permitirá efectuar un rápido progreso y además tocar con un excelente tono y sentido musical de gran calidad. El niño va a tratar de imitar al ejecutante de la grabación y así crecerá y llegará a adulto con un fino sentido musical. Es el punto más importante del trabajo en el desarrollo de su habilidad musical.

Tonalización

La palabra "tonalización" es un nuevo término acuñado para ser aplicado en el estudio de cada instrumento. Corresponde a "vocalización" del entrenamiento vocal. Su uso ha producido excelentes resultados en la educación instrumental. Tonalización es la instrucción que se da al alumno a medida que aprende cada pieza musical, para producir un bello sonido y usar una expresión musical apropiada. Debemos entrenar a los alumnos a desarrollar su oído musical para que les permita reconocer un hermoso tono y poderlo reproducir en forma similar cómo los grandes artistas del pasado y del presente.

Puntos Importantes de la Enseñanza

I. ¿Como lograr que los niños practiquen con alegría y entusiasmo? Cúal es la mejor forma de ayudarlo a disfrutar su práctica en casa.

El desafío más importante para los padres y maestros es conseguir que cada niño realice su práctica en casa con agrado y eficiencia. Ellos deben conversar sobre ésta materia, considerando y examinando cada caso para lograr un mejor éxito. Ellos deben ser motivados tomando en cuenta su propia necesidad y sentimientos.

II. La importancia de escuchar las grabaciones es vital. Haciéndolo diariamente les permitirá avanzar rápidamente. Seis dias a la semana escuchando sus cassettes más su práctica correcta serán decisivos para determinar su progreso. Esta disciplina es más importante que una o dos clases semanales.

III. El principiante debe interpretar su lección sin la partitura. Es el factor más importante para desarrollar su memoria. También le permite progresar rápidamente. Introducirlos en la lectura musical debe ser de acuerdo a su edad y capacidad. Es muy importante que aprendan la notación musical bien, pero si es forzado a tocar y leer en forma simultánea desde el comienzo de su estudio, durante sus recitales se sentirá inseguro y no podrá mostrar su verdadera habilidad musical.

Para adquirir destreza y habilidad musical se debe practicar el instrumento diariamente. Cuando el niño aprende su idioma materno la lectura sólo comienza después que ha aprendido a hablar correctamente. En el aprendizaje del instrumento musical se debe seguir el mismo ejemplo. Tocar y leer simultáneamente se enseña sólamente después de haber adquirido destreza, sensibilidad musical y desarrollo de la memoria. Al comienzo la lectura se aprende en forma separada de la técnica y la habilidad de interpretar con un hermoso tono.

IV. Cuando un alumno logra memorizar una pieza sin errores de notas y digitación, es el momento de empezar a cultivar su maestría musical. Yo le diría al niño "ahora estás listo." Podemos empezar el trabajo más importante para desarrollar tu habilidad musical, entonces se procederá a cultivar su sensibilidad artística tocando con un bello tono, un hermoso fraseo.

La calidad del recital del alumno dependerá de la constante atención del profesor sobre éstos importantes puntos musicales.

Otro aspecto muy importante es cuando el niño toca la pieza A en forma satisfactoria y se le da una nueva pieza B; él no debe dejar A sino que debe practicar A y B al mismo tiempo. Este procedimiento debe continuar a medida que se van agregando nuevas piezas. Es muy importante repasar siempre todo su repertorio para desarrollar su habilidad a un grado más alto.

V. Padres e hijos deben siempre observar clases individuales de otros alumnos. Esta es una motivación más y es muy importante. Cuando el alumno observe las clases de otros niños va a querer interpretar tan bien como ellos y su deseo de practicar en casa va a aumentar.

La extensión de cada clase debe variar de acuerdo a la necesidad de cada niño. La concentración del alumno depende de su desarrollo y la edad principalmente. Si el niño se puede concentrar por corto tiempo es mejor acortar la duración de la clase. Un día la lección puede durar cinco minutos y otro día puede ser de 30 minutos.

Es muy importante trabajar junto a los padres de los alumnos.

La presencia de los padres en cada lección es de vital importancia, pues durante la semana de práctica él estará atento a las indicaciones del profesor y podrá ayudar a su hijo, corrigiendolo y estimulándolo en forma positiva.

Shinichi Suzuki

SUZUKI METHODE FÜR BLOCKFLöTEN
NEUE UND WIRKUNGAVOLLE LEHRMETHODE

Durch die Erfahrung, die ich über die fünfzig Jahre in Lehrversuchen mit jungen Kindern gewonnen habe, bin ich zu dem definitiven Entschluss gekommen, dass musikalische Fähigkeit kein angeborenes Talent ist, sondern eine Fähigkeit, die entwickelt werden kann; jedes Kind kann mit richtiger Anleitung musikalische Fähigkeit entwickeln, geradeso wie alle Kinder dieser Welt die Fähigkeit entwickelt haben, ihre Muttersprache zu erlernen. Kinder lernen die Nuancen ihrer Muttersprache durch wiederholtes Hören und der gleiche Vorgang sollte für die Entwicklung des musikalischen Gehöres befolgt werden. Jeden Tag sollten die Kinder Tonbandaufnahmen von der Musik die sie gerade studieren oder demnächst studieren werden, anhören. Dieses Zuhören hilft ihnen zu besonders schnellem Fortschritt. Die Kinder werden ihr Bestes Versuchen so gut zu spielen wie der Spieler auf der Tonwiedergabe. Durch diese Methode wird das Kind zu einer Person mit feinem musikalischen Gehör heranwachsen. Die ist das wichtigste Training für musikalische Fähigkeit.

Tonführung

Das Wort "Tonführung" ist ein neues Wort, geschöpft zur Anwendung im Instrumentunterricht, so wie "Stimmführung" im Stimmunterricht verwendet wird. Tonführung hat wundervolle Resultate in der Instrumental-Erziehung hervorgebracht. Tonführung ist die Anweisung, die dem Schüler bei der Erlernung jedes neuen Musikstückes gegeben wird, um ihm zu helfen, einen schönen Klang und sinnvollen musikalischen Ausdruck hervorzubringen. Wir müssen den Schüler trainieren, das musikalische Gehör, das ihn befähigt, einen schonen Klang zu erkennen, zu entwickeln. Danach muss er gelehrt werden, wie er den schönen Klang und den feinen musikalischen Ausdruck alter und gegenwärtiger Klavierkünstler selbst wieder hervorbringen kann.

Wichtige Punkte für den Unterricht

I.   Die Kinder dazu anzuregen, dass ihnen das Üben Spass macht."Was ist der beste Weg, dass ein Schüler mit Freude lernt und übt?" Dies ist das grundlegende Problem für Lehrer und Eltern, wie man das Kind richtig motivieren kann, so dass es mit Freude in der richtigen Weise daheim übt. Sie sollten diese Frage gemeinsam besprechen, wobei jeder Fall insbesondere betrachtet und berücksichtigt werden muss, um dem Kind zu helfen, die Stunden und Übungen mit Freude zu betreiben. Sie sollten ein Gefühl für den Geisteszustand des Kindes haben.

II. Wenn zusätzlich zu dem täglichen Üben daheim, das Kind die Tonaufnahmen von dem Stück, das es gerade lernt, jeden Tag und so oft wie möglich anhört, so wird der Fortschritt schnell sein. Sechs Tage die Woche mit richtiger Übung und Zuhören daheim wird wesentlich mehr entscheidend für die Geschwindigkeit des Fortschrittes des Kindes sein, als ein oder zwei Unterrichtsstunden die Woche.

III. Anweisung in Notenlesen
     Der anfangende Schüler sollte immer ohne Notation in der Übungsstunde spielen. Dies ist der wichtigste Faktor für die Gedächtnis-Stärkung des Schülers. Es beschleunigt gleichzeitig des Schülers Fortschrit.

Anweisung in Notenlesen sollte dem Alter und der Fähigkeit des Schülers angepasst werden. Es ist sehr wichtig, dass der Schüler das Notenlesen gut lernt, aber wenn das Kind gleich am Anfang seines Studiums gezwungen wird, Noten zu lesen und immer nach Noten zu üben, so wird er sich bei der Vorführung aus dem Gedächtnis sehr unbehaglich fühlen und wird seine volle Fähigkeit nicht zeigen können.

In der Erwerbung einer Geschicklichkeit wächst die Fähigkeit durch tägliche Gewohnheit. In der Erlernung seiner Muttersprache beginnt das Kind mit Lesen erst nachdem es sprechen kann. Der gleiche Vorgang sollte in der Musik befolgt werden. Gleichzeitiges Spielen während des Notenlesens wird nur dann gelehrt nachdem das Kind Musikalische Sensibilität, Spielfähigkeit und Gedächtnis genügend trainiert hat. Man darf dabei jedoch nicht übersehen, dass das Notenlesen gelehrt wird, so dass die Schüler ohne Noten zu spielen lernen. Selbst nachdem sie die Fähigkeit des Notenlesens erworben haben, spielen die Kinder in der Regel im Unterricht aus dem Gedächtnis. Am Anfang wird das Notenlesen getrennt von Tonerzeugen und Instrumenten gelernt.

IV. Die Lehrmethode zur Entwicklund der Geschicklichkeit.
     Wenn ein Schüler die Stufe erreicht, wo er ein Stück ohne Fehler in Noten oder Fingersatz spielen kann, dann ist die Zeit reif, seine Künstlerschaft zu kultivieren. Ich würde zu dem Kinde sagen: "Jetzt bist Du bereit. Wir können nun mit der sehr wichtigen Aufgabe beginnen, deine Geschicklichkeit zu entwickeln." Und ich würde dann dazu übergehen, ihm einen Klang, feine Wiedergabe und musikalische Empfindsamkeit zu lehren. Die Qualität in des Schülers Vorführung hängt weitgehend von des Lehrers ständiger Aufmerksamkeit auf jene wichtigen musikalischen Punkte ab.

Der jetzt folgende Punkt ist sehr wichtig. Wenn das Kind Stück A zufriedenstellend spielen kann und ein neues Stück B zu spielen bekommt, so sollte er A nicht fallen lassen, sondern beide Stücke A und B zur gleichen Zeit weiter üben. Dieses Vorgehen sollte beibehalten werden, wenn immer neue Stücke hinzugefügt werden. Er sollte immer Stücke, die er gut kennt, wiederholen, um seine Fähigkeit in höherem Grade zu entwickeln.

V.   Einzelunterricht
     Eltern und Kinder beobachten immer die Einzelunterrichtsstunden anderer Kinder. Dies erhöht die Motivierung. Wenn das Kind andere Kinder gut spielen hört, so möchte es auch gut spielen können, und auf diese Weise wird sein Wunsch zu üben verstärkt. Die Dauer der Unterrichtsstunden sollte je nach Bedarf des Kindes wechseln. Die Aufmerksamkeits-Spanne des Kindes sollte dabei in Betracht gezogen werden. Wenn das kleine Kind sich nur für kürze Zeit kinzentrieren kann, ist es besser, die Stunde zu kürzen, bis er sich besser anpassen kann. Einmal mag der Unterricht nur fünfzig Minuten dauern, und ein andermal dreissig Minuten. Die Lehrer arbeiten mit den Eltern und Kindern.

Shinichi Suzuki

ECOLE DE FLÛTE À BEC SUZUKI
Method d'Enseignement Nouvelle et Efficace

De par l'expérience que j'ai acquise en enseignant la musique aux jeunes enfants pendant plus de cinquant ans, je suis toùt à fait convaincu que l'habilete musicale n'est pas un talent inné mais une habileté qui pent être développée. Tous les enfants correctement entrainés peuveat développer un talent musical de la même manière que tous les enfants du monde développent peu à peu une habileté à parler leur langue maternelle. Les enfants apprennent les nuances de leur langue maternelle à force d'écouter bien des fois cette langue, et le méme procédé devrait avoir lieu dans le développement de leur oreille musicale. Tous les jours, les enfants devraient écouter les enregistrements des morceaux qu'ils sont en train d'étudier ou qu'ils vont étudier. Cette audition les aide à faire de rapides progrès. Les enfants commenceront à essayer de leur mieux à jouer aussi bien que l'exécutant au disque. Avec cette méthode l'enfant developera un sens musical raffiné. Ceci est l'élément le plus important dans la formation de l'habileté musicale.

Tonalisation

Le mot "tonlisation" est un nouveau mot introduit dans l'étude des instruments comparable au mot "vocalisation" dans l'étude du chant. Les exercices de tonalisation ont donnés de très bons résultats dans l'education instrumentale. La tonalisation est l'instruction donnée à l'élève chaque fois qu'il apprend un nouveau morceau de musique; instruction destinée à l'aider à produire un beau ton et une expression musicale intelligente et expressive. Nous devons former l'élève afin qu'il développe une oreille musicale apte à reconnaître un beau ton. On doit alors lui enseigner à reproduire les beaux tons et les expressions musicales de qualité des viruoses du passé et du présent.

Enseignement: Points Importants

I. Comment Faire les Enfants Prendre Plaisir à Pratiqer
Quelle est la meilleure façon d'aider un élève à prendre du plaisir à apprendre et à pratiquer? Ceci est le défi principal pour les professeurs et les parents: motiver l'enfant de telle sorte qu'il prenne du plaisir à pratiquer correctement à la maison. Ils devraient discuter de ce sujet ensemble en considérant et en examinant chaque cas particulier, ceci afin d'aider l'enfant à prendre du plaisir aux lecons et aux exercises. Ils devraient considérer les sensibilités de l'enfant.

II. L'Importance de l'Audition des Disques
Si l'élève, en plus de son travail quotidien à la maison, écoute tous les jours et aussi souvent que possible, l'enregistrement des morceaux qu'il apprend, les progrès seront rapides. Six jours par semaine de pratique correct et d'audition à la maison seront plus déterminants pour les progrès de l'enfant qu'une ou deux leçons par semaine.

III. L'Instruction dans la Lecture des Notes
Pèndant les leçons l'élève novice devrait toujours jouer sans partition. Ceci est très important pour le développement de la mémoire de l'élève et accélère les progrès. Au début, les indications des notes sont apprises séparément de la production des tons et la technique instrumentale.

L'Enseignement de la lecture des notes devrait être donné en fonction de l'àge et de l'aptitude de l'élève. Il est très important pour l'élève d'apprendre à lire correctement la musique, mais si l'enfant est forcé à lire la musique, dès la début de son étude, et s'il practique toujours avec une partition, il se sentira mal à l'aise quand il faudra jouer de mémoire et par conséquent ne pourra pas montrer son habileté au maximum.

Dans tout apprentissage l'habileté croît grâce à un entrainement journalier. Lorsque l'enfant apprend sa langue maternelle, il ne commence à lire que lorsqu'il est capable de parler. La même approche devrait être suivie en musique. Jouer et simultanément lire la musique n'est enseigné que lorsque la sensibilité musicale de l'enfant son habileté à jouer et sa mémoire son suffisament entrainés.

IV. La Méthode d'Enseignement pour Développer l'Habileté
Quand un élève atteint un niveau où il peut jouer un morceau sans erreur de doigter ou de note, il est mûr pour développer l'art musical. Je dirais à l'enfant, "maintenant que tu es prêt, nous pouvons commencer le travail très important qui consiste à développer ton habileté," puis je lui apprendrais à trouver un beau ton, un phrase de qualité et une bonne sensibilité musicale. La qualité des exécutions de l'élève dépend largement de l'attention constante portée par le professeur à ces points musicaux essentiels.

Le point suivant est très important. Quand l'enfant peut jouer de manière satisfaisante un composition. A et qu'il reçoit un nouveau composition B, il ne devrait pas abandonner le composition A, mais il devrait pratiquer les deux compositions. Ceci devrait continuer quand de nouveaux sont ajoutés. Il devrait toujours répéter les compositions qu'il connaît afin de développer son habileté a un plus haut degré.

V. Leçon Individuelles
Les parents et les enfants eux mêmes devraient toujours assister aux leçons individuelles des autres enfants. Ceci constitue une autre motivation. Quand un enfant entend une musique bien jouée par un autre enfant, il voudra être capable de la jouer aussi bien, ainsi son désir de pratiquer augmentera-t-il.

La durée des leçons devrait varier en fonction des besoins de l'enfant, on devrait considérer la faculté d'attention de l'enfant. Si un jeune enfant ne peut se concentrer que pendant un court moment, il vaut mieux raccourcir la durée de la leçon. Une leçon peut parfois durer cinq minutes et d'autres fois trente minutes. Les professeurs travaillent avec les parents et les enfants.

Shinichi Suzuki

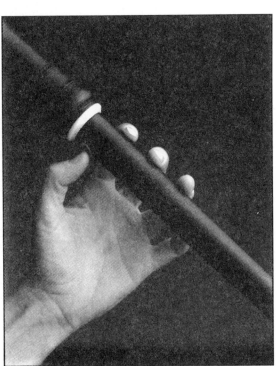

Note the left thumb position for the upper register tone, and the relaxed embouchure, with lip corners inward.

A flexible embouchure is ideal. When you play the middle and upper registers, the area surrounding the mouth frequently becomes more balloon-shaped. There is a cushion of air under the nose, between the front teeth and inner lip surface.

When the left thumb needs to be completely off the thumb hole, keep it very close to the thumb hole so it will be ready to close the thumb hole entirely, or to "half-hole" for an upper register tone.

The left thumbnail is kept short.

Use only a slight left thumb pressure to cover the thumb hole because the left thumb needs to move with flexibility.

When we "half-hole" we maintain light contact with the thumb-hole perimeter. The size of the thumb hole opening (aperture) usually varies. In this case the thumb covers less of the thumb hole.

In this case more of the thumb hole is covered. The angle at the thumb joint depends on the thumb length, and on the various positions required as we play. To develop efficient technique, carefully practice the thumb movements required to change positions. The wrist remains stable.

Tonalization

Larghetto ♩ = 60

A

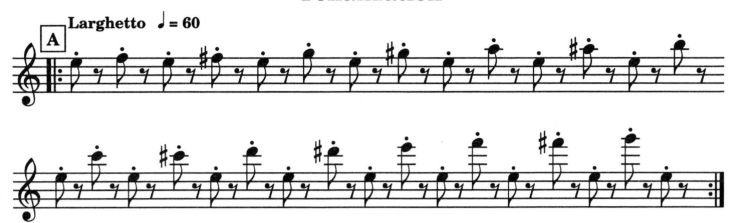

B **Larghetto**

Play with tongued legato, i.e. Du- Du-, Tu- Du-, and slur to D.

Larghetto

C

Tongued legato.

10

Play with a smooth connection.

Play with dynamic accents.

*In this example the trill begins on the upper neighbor. The upper neighbor is included in the first two pieces as a reminder for you. This preliminary higher tone is generally assumed in Baroque style, except in fast passages.

Simplified trill with preparation on the beat of the principal tone.

Preparatory Studies

∥ means stop...prepare...play.

1

The Flowers Are Sleeping

Folk Song

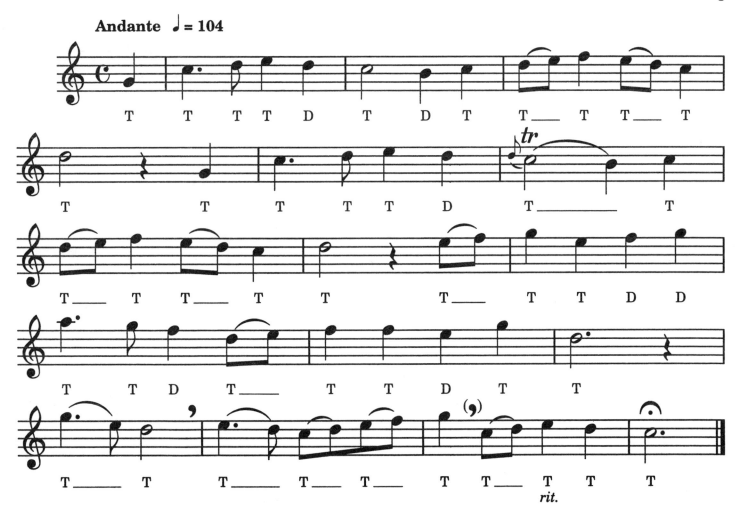

Preparatory Studies

2

The Silent Moon

Folk Song

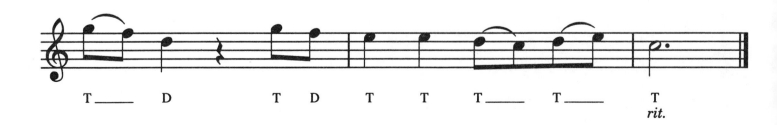

Preparatory Studies

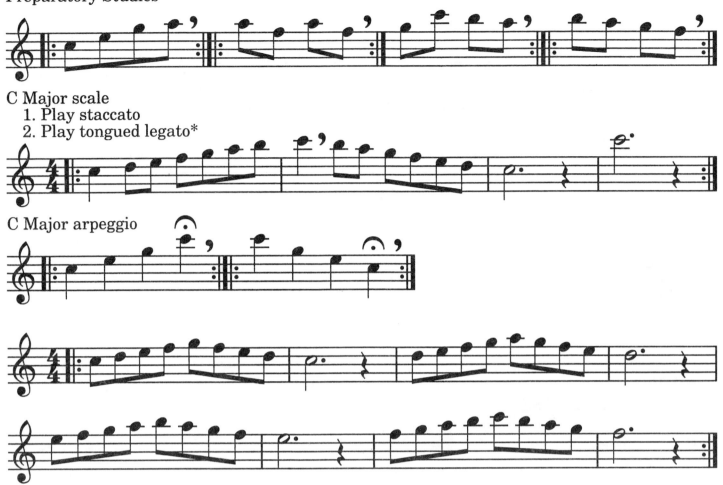

C Major scale
1. Play staccato
2. Play tongued legato*

C Major arpeggio

*Tongued legato: The air stream is interrupted very slightly with a tiny motion of the tongue tip.
The separation between the tones is minimal.

3

Early One Morning

Folk Song

Moderato ♩ = 104

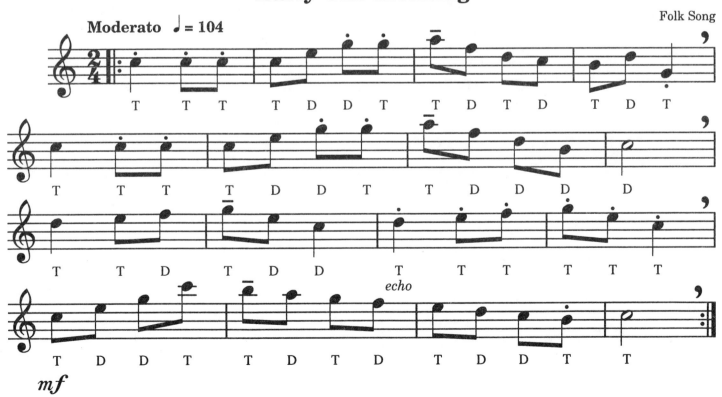

mf

Five-tone sequences

Preparatory study

Written

Played approximately

4

Siciliana
from Sonata in F Major

G. F. Handel
Op. 1, No. 11

D Minor scales and arpeggio

Preparatory Studies

Emphasize the appogiatura.
Make a smooth connection.

5

Menuet in D Minor
from Suite No. 2 in B Minor

J. S. Bach

Allegretto ♩ = 104

1. 2nd time:

F Major scale and arpeggio

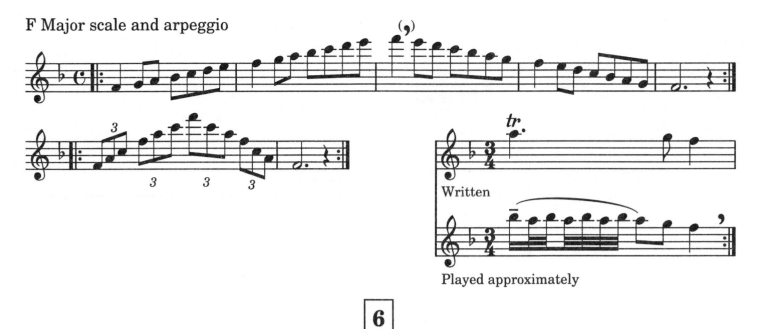

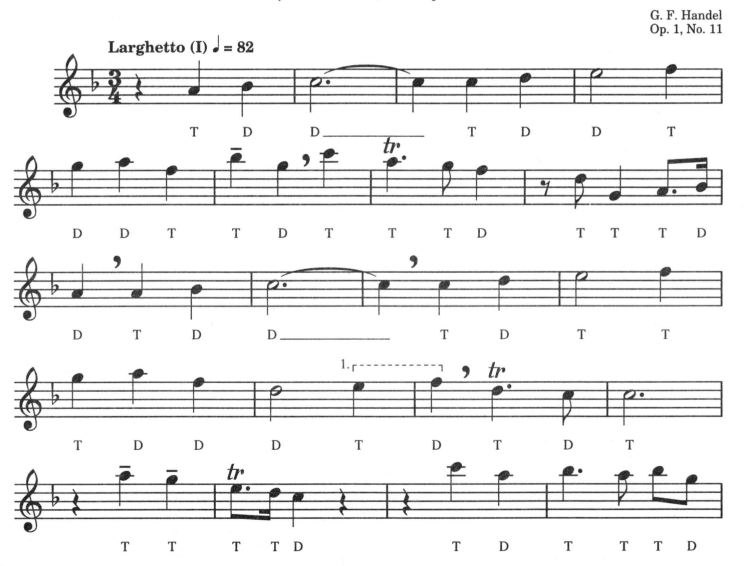

6

Larghetto
from Sonata in F major

G. F. Handel
Op. 1, No. 11

1. ⌐‾‾‾‾‾‾¬ = hemiola. Make an audible change from 3 beats to 2 beats.

T D D D T T T D T T T T T T T

T D T T D T T D T T T D T T T T T T

D T D D T D T D D T D D

T D T T T T T T T T T T

T D T T T D T D T T D T T T

D T T D T D T T D

rit.

18

These are some techniques we can use to influence volume (dynamics):

Softer volume or echo

1. Less tonal length.

2. Direct the wind toward the first hole.

3. Use "piano fingerings". These fingerings would be too sharp with normal wind speed, but they will result in proper intonation when played with less wind speed. The tone is less resonant as well.

Louder volume

1. More tonal length.

2. Direct the wind down toward the bell.

3. Cover all or part of another recorder hole as you increase the wind speed.

Special, alternate fingerings depend on your particular instrument, and are chosen with the advice of your teacher according to each situation with your level in mind.

B♭ Major scale and arpeggio

Preparatory Studies

Detached style

Bourrée in B♭ Major
from The Water Music Suite

G. F. Handel

Play ♫ rhythmically.

Allegro tongue (attack): This kind of articulation promotes a lively, joyful, spirited character.

Play several times as you whisper "Tu," and withdraw your tongue tip *quickly* from your palate, just behind your upper front teeth.

G Minor scales and arpeggio

Harmonic

Melodic

8

Larghetto
from Sonata in G Minor

G. F. Handel
Op. 1, No. 2

Larghetto (I) ♪ = 88

T   D   D____ D   T

T   R   D   T   T   D   D   T   D   D   T

*Prepare the trill by prolonging the upper neighbor preceding the principal tone.
The beginning of the trill is delayed in this case.

9

Bourrée in G Minor
from the Royal Fireworks Suite

G. F. Handel

A minor scales and arpeggios

10

Menuet in A minor
from Suite No. 4 in E minor

C. Dieupart

11

March in F Major
BWV Anh. 122

C. P. E. Bach

12

Presto
from Sonata in G Minor

G. F. Handel
Op. 1, No. 2

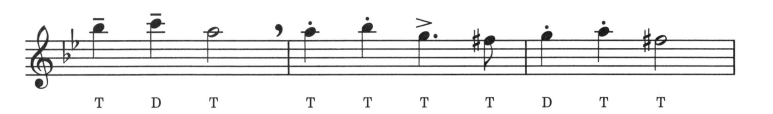

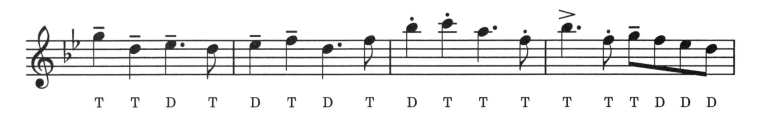

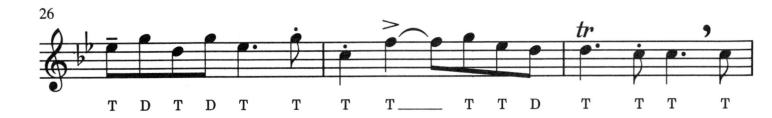

Bourrée in F Major (Harmony Part)
from The Water Music Suite

G. F. Handel
Op. 1, No. 2

This is an optional harmony part which may be played when a C instrument plays the melody. (See Soprano Recorder Volume 2.)

Bourrée in D Minor (Harmony Part)
from the Royal Fireworks Suite

G. F. Handel

This is an optional harmony part which may be played when a C instrument plays the melody. (See Soprano Recorder Volume 3.)